TRIUMPH HOUSE
Poetry with a Purpose

GIGGLE IN THE WIND

Edited by

Kelly Oliver

First published in Great Britain in 2002 by
TRIUMPH HOUSE
Remus House,
Coltsfoot Drive,
Peterborough, PE2 9JX
Telephone (01733) 898102

All Rights Reserved

Copyright Contributors 2002

HB ISBN 1 90422 048 7
SB ISBN 1 90422 049 5

FOREWORD

Today, poetry has become a more recognisable form of expression and communication. Different styles are used by different authors, and from traditional to contemporary, all are included in this carefully and well thought-out anthology.

Over 100 new and established writers featured in *Giggle In The Wind* share their thoughts, feelings and views with you, the reader.

With some of the best poetry emerging today, we assure you that this book is an exciting and inspiring joy to be read time and time again.

Kelly Oliver
Editor

CONTENTS

Your Last Day	Susan Turner	1
Private Ward	Peter Huggins	2
Mary And Bill	Shoshanna Fletcher	3
Mom's Favourite Cake	Lola Perks-Hartnell	4
Legend	Ursula Kiernan	5
The Great Book	Dawna Mechelle	6
Who Tires First?	Jean C Pease	7
Remoulds	A Marten	8
On Fire!	Paddy Jupp	9
Some Cross Words	G Rogers	10
Bird Unheard	E Balmain	11
Face Cream, One Missing	M E Smith	12
Animal Magic	Trevor Napper	13
Samson And Delilah	Nicola Barnes	14
I Will Always Love You	Janet Hickling	15
Lost In A Dream	Eduardo Del-Rio Escalona	16
The Happy Gardener	Peg Ritchie	18
Unknown Follower	A Odger	19
The Union Of Material	Gerard Craven	20
Our National Health Service	Stan Gilbert	22
Anecdote By Poem	B Frost	23
A Long Twisted Tale	Margaret Lightbody	24
Spanish Political Tragedy	Mick Nash	25
Nectarine	Bah Kaffir	26
1943	S Glover	27
It Ghosts To Show	Margaret B Baguley	28
All Their Plans Dispersed	S Mullinger	29
The Performer	H D Hensman	30
Shopping	Pam Owers	31
Discovery	Frank Howarth-Hynes	32
Knowing One's Place	Myra Bowen	33
Stood Up By My Umbrella	Charles David	34
Where's The Town Centre?	Leonard Jeffries	36
Temptation	Ann G Wallace	37
The One That Got Away	Daphne McFadyen	38
I'm In Love	M J Morgan	39

Dark Black Coat	Susan Lewis	40
Black Narcissus	Ian Barton	41
At Last You Found Me	Jodie McKane	42
Who's Who?	John Napier Williams	43
The Stone Lion	Caroline Ayre	44
The Balance Of Nature	Barry Langley	45
Plague	Jeffrey A Pickford	46
Capitalism	Jay Baker	47
Rude Awakening	J Howling Smith	48
Friends	Joyce Walker	49
Dejected	J A Silkstone	50
Mystery Trip	Joy Saunders	51
The Pixie's Party	Violetta J Ferguson	52
The Perfect Pair	Molly M Hamilton	53
Epitaphs	Jack Bowden	54
Pie In The Sky	Maurice Ivor Birch	55
A Schoolboy's Dream	Harry Gill	56
Encounter	Patricia M Ponting	57
Hazard Of Oz	Erchin Diss	58
The Hapy Wanderer	Ethel Wakeford	59
An Early Date	J Aldred	60
The Gift	E M Eagle	61
The Mouse	Louise Mills	62
I Can Be	Ise Obomhense	63
Copresence	Michael C Soper	64
Harley Street	G H Bryant	65
Our Lasting Roses	Lesley J Worrall	66
A Time To Play	Heather Breadnam	67
Lost My Mind	Charles David Jenkins	68
Guess Who	Joyce Hammond	69
Almost One Of The Family	Freda Grieve	70
Bedtime Sounds	Deborah Grimwade	71
I Am Beautiful	Hilary Jill Robson	72
Snowflakes	Jean Caldwell	73
Tube Line	Lesley Vann	74
My Bike	Francis Joseph Lawton	75
Stay With Me	Linda Cooper	76
Who Killed My Brother?	Andrew Brian Zipfell	77

The Call	Kristina Howells	78
Beans For Supper	Gloria Hargreaves	79
The Last Dance	Jonathan Covington	80
My Life Without You	Helen Legg	81
The Silent Army	Jean M Wood	82
Nineteen	Andrew Detheridge	83
The Dark Horse	Margaret Gleeson Spanos	84
Spinster's Song	Sarah Blackmore	85
Moving House Madness	Lindsey Brown	86
A Fence Too Far	Catherine Armstrong	87
Tea Without	Graham K A Walker	88
A Sense Of Humour	D A Sheasby	89
That Certain Age	Leslie Holgate	90
Jumped Off	Margaret Upson	91
Limerick	Alan Pow	92
Hay Fever	Mary Skelton	93
Fun	E Riggott	94
Lady From Bude	Molly Mettam	95
Office Politics	Anna Gillions	96
More Adventures With Santa Claus	Jean P Edwards McGovern	97
Wrapping Presents	A J Renyard	98
Jungle Tales	Linda Ann Johnson	99
Our Dog	Jim Sargant	100
Baby Sister	Philip Buist	101
Pudding Lame	Jean Paisley	102
Reflections On A Journey	Terry Daley	103
Vale Of Tears	Norman Bissett	104
Shocking Swim	Geoffrey Woodhead	105
Dot	Ethel Napper	106
Whoops	Edmund Hyde	107
RIP	Joyce Hockley	108
Samson	Roma Davies	109
At Home With Holmes	R L Cooper	110
2773	H G Griffiths	111
Cat's Days	Roger Brooks	112
Infinity	Stan Downing	113
Over The Hill	Stuart Delvin	114

Untitled	GBC	115
The Dentist	Ann Dempsey	116
Demons	Kimberly Harries	117
Miss Maggie Macgree	B Clarke	118
The Christmas Party	Julia L Holden	119
A Lesson	M MacDonald-Murray	120
Beyond Credence	Corinne Lovell	121
Sweet Brown Bear	Helen Owen	122
Finished Starter	Robert D Shooter	123
The Remedy	D M Carne	124
Party Mayhem	Hazell Dennison	125
Bright Colours Of Youth	Sonia Riggs	126
Time On My Hands	Kath Barber	127
Monks Eleigh	Richard Lee Nettleton	128
Chip-Monk	Robert John Moore	130
The Man From The Isle Of Wight	Val Spall	131
The Robin	Matthew L Burns	132
Rasputin Made Me Miss My Bus!	Jonathan Goodwin	133
Old Companions	Brian Bates	134
The Diet	Christine Lannen	135
The Rookie	Linda Zulaica	136
You're Sunk Mate!	Roger Williams	137
Jed's Parrot	Mary Wood	138
Give That Tune The Brush Off!	Rosina L Gutcher	139
The Wedding	Peter Arthur Butcher	140
Go On! Just One More!	Angela Jones	141
The Boar	Valerie Ovais	142
A Twist To The Tale	Ellen Thompson	143

YOUR LAST DAY

Your friendship I have valued,
and your kindness too;
the tears of laughter, many,
the tears of heartache, few.
But I've never known it hurt me
to say goodbye each day,
hear your door shut swiftly,
nor watch you walk away,
                quite like today.

Susan Turner

PRIVATE WARD

He's plaster-casted, feeling blue.
A rich man in a private ward
surveys the world from window view
of passing traffic, really bored.

Impatient patient clocks them all
for someone special's on her way.
A lovely lady svelte and tall
who waves at him and makes his day.

Cured at last, he walks the pavement,
looks back to see his vacant shack,
waves goodbye, to his amazement,
some fifty windows answer back.

Peter Huggins

MARY AND BILLY

Mary Muckle and Billy Bray were born the same time on the same day, the other side of the street some would say, were Mary Muckle and Billy Bray.

Billy grew up loved, for him no struggle, it wasn't the same for Mary Muckle. Born to filth and squalor was she, yet from within shone a rare beauty.

A politician did Billy become, well thought of by everyone
But a troubled mind did Billy have, what was it like for others to live?
So down the hill he went one day, some said it was the end for Billy Bray, but the beginning for Mary Muckle, I'd say.

Down the hill each day he would come, Billy Bray, the politician's son, to meet the daughter of one unknown, but to Billy it was like coming home.

To the beach one day they did go, how it quite happened no one knows, except the two themselves in love, decided it was time to leave this world, Mary Muckle and Billy Bray were found in each other's arms that day, leaving the Earth as they came.

Looking down on Billy Bray, stood a man broken-hearted at the loss of this day, his son and daughter taken away.
No one to share with him his grief, two worlds pulled together had shattered his dreams.

Shoshanna Fletcher

MOM'S FAVOURITE CAKE

My mother thought she'd like to bake
Her usual 'tip-top' family cake,
Taking her usual painstaking care
All the ingredients to prepare.

The recipe, of course, she knew by heart,
Just as easy as making jam tart,
Enjoyed so many times before,
Always with a loud 'encore'.

Smoothly mixing the familiar batter,
Oblivious to all distraction and chatter,
She popped it in the oven - put up her feet,
Mentally tasting the longed-for treat!

Success guaranteed, she had no fear,
The smell of it cooking, gave her cheer,
But alas! When she opened the oven door,
The cake had collapsed all over the floor!
Nevertheless, she scooped it all up,
Putting the smaller bits into a cup.
She served it at tea as an 'accident cake',
Folk voted it scrumptious, and asked her to bake
Another for next time they came to tea,
But she can't make it now for love, nor money,
For a home-made *accident* you can't connive,
It won't happen to order, however you strive!

Mom's home-made *now* is a family joke,
But she really *once* had the *professional* stroke!

Lola Perks-Hartnell

LEGEND

I never liked Dorothy much. Or her pale fawn pug
with its gross behind. Every Sunday's the same,
when there's so much else we could do with the time.
She has everything here she could possibly need.

The place is as good as Butlin's, what with bingo
and quizzes, regular outings; Darby and Joans.
One nurse is a right little cracker. She's asked me
if I work out! There are times I wish I was single.

Dorothy's life is over. We've spent our inheritance
time and again in our heads. Disney Land for the kids.
Early retirement. A better car. Meanwhile, we talk
of incontinence pads, cataracts, toenails and such.

But there's only one topic that interests her now:
'How's my Dodo today?' We keep his legend alive:
his sexual exploits, his battles with cats, the missing
chicken, the pork chops and cream he's scoffed.

Just as we're off, she thanks us again for our kindness
to Dodo and asks 'Couldn't you bring him to see me
one day?' We smile saying Matron would never
allow it: the truth is we had him put down long ago.

Ursula Kiernan

THE GREAT BOOK

'A divided race once existed, called human beings.
Divided by religion.
Each religious union believed they were the ultimate choice.
Translating the book into many different languages.
They refused to accept that our great emperor,
On his last visit to Earth, had accidentally left the book behind.
When he returned to collect it,
They insisted that he was the second coming.'

Dawna Mechelle

WHO TIRES FIRST?

The children took Bobby their dog for a walk
On a beautiful summer's day,
They decided to take him down to the beach,
Where they could all romp and play.
A stick was thrown for Bobby to fetch -
He loved carrying it back for more,
But the children got tired before the dog,
Before long they found it a bore.
How could they stop this monotonous game?
Bobby seemed to enjoy it so well,
He barked incessantly for the stick to be thrown
As though he were under a spell.
Then David had a brilliant idea
As they walked towards the sea,
Bobby hated his bath - so he'd hate getting wet,
So the stick was thrown to the water with glee.
Alas for the children the tide was coming in
And Bobby from the ocean got help,
He barked and barked until in a short while
He picked up the stick with an excited yelp.
No need to get wet - apart from his paws,
And that he didn't mind at all -
So the children had to think of another game,
As - tired out - on the sand they did fall.

Jean C Pease

REMOULDS

Have you ever thought of your body
And how it grows every day?
Repairing each part is really an art
So many things come into play.

Of course you live in your body
But is it really on loan?
Perhaps the rent's overdue now
Better get on the phone.

Could be you could do with a trade-in
Sometimes it's the best thing to do
Who knows you might get a slim-line
But you'll have to get in the queue.

The storeman's really quite busy
Though he has a computer to help
But even a second-hand body
Is better than one on the shelf.

If your present one's fading quite fast
And you feel your need is that great
Oh no, they've gone ex-directory!
Well isn't that really just fate?

A Marten

ON FIRE!

My legs go round like piston rings
As I race along the miles
With my feet glued to the pedals
And my face all wreathed in smiles.

For I know I'm getting better
'Cause my legs aren't full of lead
Like they were when I first started -
But the pounds don't seem to shed!

Now I'll have a go at rowing
For they say that's jolly tough
And they're right, after ten minutes
I have really had enough.

But I've got to keep on going
As it's great to exercise
Though I can't get too exhausted -
It might lead to my demise!

Now there's trampolining still to go
And wobbly boarding too -
Oh joy! The physiotherapist's said
'Now that's enough for you!'

But I'm on fire, feel fighting fit,
This exercise is fun,
So I'll jog off home, for after all
I'm only *ninety-one!*

Paddy Jupp

SOME CROSS WORDS
(A true story)

A lady vicar, newly ordained
Asked where a cross could be obtained
Could I make one on a stand
That could be carried in her hand?

I made her one ten inches high
The wood was solid mahogany
She said, when the varnish was really dry
It was very pleasing to touch and see.

Other people asked for some more
The total rose to twenty-four
In the church, one three feet high
Others, quite small, caught their eye.

Some exotic woods came my way
And the crosses increased day by day
Five hundred, and five hundred more
Deep in shavings, my shed floor.

People in hospitals, found them soothing
Demand kept production moving
Fifteen hundred, had now been passed
'The Cross Man', Me, I'd been typecast.

Many have gone to foreign lands
Bringing joy to Christian hands
My own ambition for what it's worth
One for each year of Jesus' birth.

That achievement has now been done
Crosses number two thousand and one
My grand-daughter helped, she was quite good
She now has that cross of white holly wood.

__G Rogers__

BIRD UNHEARD

We were out in the country - a beautiful day.
The air was quite sharp but the sun bade us stay.
As we strolled by the hedge, along the roadside,
Through a gap in the bush, a pond we espied.
'Oh hush! Just don't move!' I said to my friend.
I think she was sure that I'd gone round the bend!
But I pointed my finger to show her a sight,
A motionless heron standing just to the right;
Its feet in the water, no movement it made . . .
Nor did we, as we whispered 'Don't make it afraid.'
Along a path in the distance, there suddenly appeared
A farmer, watching us as if we were weird.
He beckoned us to come, so we tiptoed past the bird.
It didn't move a feather, and we uttered not a word.
As we reached the farmer, I explained why we were quiet,
And he guffawed so much, we thought he'd start a riot!
'Frighten yon big bird! Now that would be quite drastic.
You couldn't move it not one jot. The durn thing's made of plastic!'

E Balmain

FACE CREAM, ONE MISSING

My daughter gave me face cream
Said use it twice a day
For it really smoothes one's skin
And keeps wrinkles at bay
So for three days I tried it
Twice daily as was told
But no one seemed to notice
So I thought I would be bold
'Has no one seen a difference
On my face since I put this cream on?'
And my grand-daughter piped up loudly
'Yes Granny, one wrinkle has gone.'

M E Smith

ANIMAL MAGIC

I met her at the local park, her eyes were baby blue,
With long sensuous lashes, this was something new.

As she brushed against me, my nose had a feast,
Of her musky perfume, from the mystic east.

She had two protuberances, long and shapely legs,
Yet she would not come to the cinema, however much I begged.

She blissfully ignored me, but that was nothing new.
Her name was *Camilla* the *camel* at our local zoo.

Trevor Napper

SAMSON AND DELILAH

Samson was a strong man,
When all this began.
He had a weakness
For all his meekness:
His hair, his hair, his hair;
Scalped by Delilah though.
He tore down the temple so.

Nicola Barnes

I WILL ALWAYS LOVE YOU

You moped around like a little boy
As though looking for a long-lost toy.
You put on your shirt you ironed so well
And fastened it up as the silence fell.

'I love you' I was longing to say
But how could I, especially today.
For you lost a friend you loved so much
From today she's gone, gone for good.

I watch you, your head in your hands
Why you lost her, you can't understand.
I wish there was something I could do
I wanted to hold and comfort you.

You wipe your tears that fall once more.
Put on your coat and walk to the door.
You look at the room you'd shared together
I knew then that your love would be forever.

I went to the window to watch you still.
Your got into the hearse against your will.
I wish I could have told you, in this time I spent
How I longed for your touch and how I felt.

You can't see me now, as I'm not there
But I'm trying hard to tell you I care.
You're burying my body but not my soul
I will find a way of letting you know!

Janet Hickling

LOST IN A DREAM

Once there was a boy
Who walked the countryside
Amazed at the high mountains
Kissing the blue skies

Breathing the freedom of nature
He criss-crossed forests and streams
Searching for something hidden
A dream, was calling for him

When he wasn't a boy anymore
He adventured into the unknown
On iron wings he flew . . .
Roaming the world above

He wandered dawns and declines
Leaving his safe nest behind
Held on to family ties
Afraid of the depths he would find

Soon enough seas and continents
Were the bridges to his past
Intent on seeking that dream
Thought to be hidden on the far side

Hardships entered his life
Unveiling this pitiless world
Shattering his hopes and his trust
Difficult for him to understand

He realised that all dreams
Were at the reach of one's hand
Without distance, without absence
Without confusion, or losses to find

There was no need to conquer
Worlds beyond his child playground
No need to leave the loved ones
Wondering about his life
No need for sorrows and cries
To fulfil one's haunted heart.

Eduardo Del-Rio Escalona

THE HAPPY GARDENER

Ned the gardener leans his bike
Against the side wall of 'The Crown',
Then settles in a comfy chair
To drink a pint of Mild and Brown.

Just out of reach behind the bar
As usual, Angie reigns supreme.
With smiling eyes and rosy cheeks -
A veritable gardener's dream.

Tomorrow needs an early start
With 'pricking out' and 'potting on'.
He drains his glass, pulls on his cap
And with a little wave is gone.

He rides off down the country lane
Then puts his cycle in the shed.
Winds up the clock, puts out the cat
And soon is dozing, warm in bed.

Cocoa in hand she tiptoes in
And snuggles down beneath the covers.
Wed twenty years, it's nice to know -
Angie and Ned are lovers.

Peg Ritchie

UNKNOWN FOLLOWER

Late night shopping finished at last,
I hurried out to get home fast,
avoiding the crowds rushing past.

Glancing at windows on the way,
seeing all the goods on display,
pleased they're shut for another day.

Wondering where the children are,
wishing that home was not so far,
envious of those with a car.

A sudden feeling of unease,
causing a trembling in my knees,
tightly holding onto my keys.

Seeing a shadow on the wall,
I start to run, afraid I'll fall,
must try to hide, no one to call.

Trapped, I turn, heart pounding with dread,
and wonder why he smiles instead,
'You dropped your purse,' is all he said.

A Odger

THE UNION OF MATERIAL

Good evening, I'm Bert from the Union of Tin
And to be works convenor ain't no sin.
It's not a Union for workers, like Fred or Sam,
But the Union of the material that makes the humble can.

You don't seem to appreciate our versatile use
And us humble cans, we suffer all sorts of abuse.
We're used as a vehicle for the Nation's food,
If we had rights, then you'd all be sued.

You mangle and form us in gruesome machines,
You show us no kindness; you're just bloody mean.
When we've been through that process and you've
Knocked us about,
Your bloody machine just spits us out.

You split up our families, I'm one of twelve,
You throw us in boxes and stack us on shelves.
You toss us in trolleys and stick stamps on our head,
That's the part that most of us dread.

You put us in cupboards for days at a time,
We have no voice so we can't moan and whine.
Then, there's the moment that each of us dread,
You take us from the cupboard and smack in our head.

You pour out our contents into a pan
Then send us to live in a dirty trash can.
We do our job; we carry your food,
But, you show us no love,
You're just bloody rude.

I've come to plead with you people,
'Please, please, don't be so rude,'
We'll do our job and carry your food.
Treat us with kindness and loving care,
We're here to help and your life to share.

But, if you abuse us and continue to misuse us,
Well, we'll bring in our contingency plans,
We'll all cease to trust and we'll all turn to rust
And you'll have to carry your food in your hands.

Gerard Craven

OUR NATIONAL HEALTH SERVICE

I tossed and turned all night long, my body was racked with pain,
I felt so ill it seemed I dare not lay down my head again,
I picked up the telephone and spoke to the doctor on call,
She told me to go back to sleep, she wasn't bothered at all,
She said 'Go to the surgery tomorrow, now don't be too late,
If you call early you'll get an appointment, call about half-past eight.'
I struggled to the bathroom to try to find myself a pill,
Anything will do, I thought, so I wouldn't feel so ill,
At eight-thirty on the dot I gave the surgery a ring,
The receptionist was inquisitive so I explained everything,
She said 'Our doctors are busy people, they have so much to do,
They haven't got time to waste seeing people with colds like you,
I can give you an appointment to see him in three weeks' time,
But I'm sure by then you will be well and feeling in your prime.'
I took up the appointment, struggled to the chemist that day,
I'll go through anything, I thought, to take the pain away.
The chemist said 'I really can't prescribe anything for you,
If you take my advice you'll see your doctor before this day is through.'
I knew it was no use arguing to get the doctor to see my head,
So I went home once again and flopped into my bed,
I suffered agony and pain until the appointment date was due,
Struggled to the doctor's surgery, waited until he called me through.
He took one look at me and said 'Why have you left it so long?
The problem you have got has a hold on your body so strong,
There's nothing I can think of that I can do for you,
You should have been in hospital at least three weeks ago.

Stan Gilbert

ANECDOTE BY POEM

You either laugh or cry
Or stare at walls think of time gone by
Or tap your feet in hesitation
Or think of past many relation
Or think of times that were hard
Lost your job, got your card
Or remember children growing from birth
Thinking it was a time well-worth
Or past holidays or buying things for house
Thinking of the years with married spouse
But the postman is the main thought in mind
Is it today he will deliver answers and be kind?
Life has been cruel for a while
All you yearn for is once again to smile
Times of bad plus hate wedged in mind
Have been there trying happy path to find
Looking at watch and clock ticking fast
Should you contact who dealt with your task?
Is it not today when end and start
A new outlook for your heart?
You look at phone, should you dial
Or should you wait a little while?
You see from the window postman walking
Oh, you sign, he has stopped and is talking
Minutes seem hours before he comes to door
Letters clatter all over the floor
Looking at envelopes that have come from where
Opening the one, running fingers into hair
Yes, it has arrived, sweating you read your fate

'Your divorce decree absolute', it does state.

B Frost

A Long Twisted Tale

He had such a short time on Earth
This one man, I bring to your attention
He lived in no splendour, either I read
He lived more in poverty, indeed,
His father and mother, of King David's seed
That Davinic line, so important to us, mortals in time
He was in grave danger, this child, as a child
Born to a maiden, so meek and so mild, He
Born of a virgin, a Jewess, not defiled by man
But this was all part, and of the greatest on Earth, Master Plan.
This child did grow into manhood, and lo, he was in
favour with both God and man
Now comes the time when we begin to see, this one man,
Move to do what? Con us if he can?
Or more, but plan, this world to take over? Be a
Hitler, or a Nazi, as in the dreaded Gestapo too?
No! Not ever, for he did show what? That God is ever
on the throne, and he our very souls does, seek to
save and own, and that forever
Hence this man, the Christ, God's perfect plan, did
also heal, and raise the dead, and God's pure love, to
sinner man here, instead, seek but to reveal, to all
kind and true, forgiving too, healing all who came to him
to be true
And yet what twisted minds were at work, against him too?
His tale is told, that gospel story, now all of 2000 years old
A twist in the end tale, that has to be told, of how
he had to die, but all to save us, the dying you and I,
as man's mind surely did cross him out, there on
Calvary, without a doubt, this Saviour, and of this
most twisted world, and dare I shout, Christ Jesus!

Margaret Lightbody

SPANISH POLITICAL TRAGEDY

The leaders of the Basques of Northern Spain
Sought peaceful means to try t'achieve their aim,
They booked a big posh hotel in Madrid,
To talk about what needed to be did:
They being simple country folk at heart,
Madrid's luxury gave them quite a start,
Such magic things they'd never known before,
Like the hotel's huge revolving door:
The dining room was oh, so very swish!
Between them, they tried nearly every dish.

When, in the night, the hotel caught on fire,
They all rushed down the stairs in panic dire!
There never had been such a rush before,
They all got stuck in the revolving door:
So then, the brave hotel commissionaire
Came to their rescue, showing courage rare,
He charged the door with strength he'd never showed,
And all the Basques shot out into the road:
The night-time traffic being still quite thick,
A few poor sods got killed off pretty quick,
The moral of this tale is one of wit,
Don't put all your Basques in one exit!

Mick Nash

NECTARINE

Nectarine so beautiful,
Delightful when in blush,
Skin so smooth, flesh so tender,
Like the singing of a thrush,
Radiant she displays herself,
Tempting me to touch.
She decorates my garden
In the sunshine and the hush,
And as I gaze upon my dream
It fills me with delight,
So creative, yet so sad,
For Nectarine would be my daughter,
The daughter I never had!

Bah Kaffir

1943

One night I got on a strange flight,
as it left the ground there was no sound.
We took off and flew to another dimension,
a UFO passed by that got our attention.
We travelled far, far away
where we landed I cannot say.
We stayed there for a while,
some took pictures asking people to smile.
When we got back aboard our plane,
we returned from whence we came.
Touching down things were not as they should be,
the year was nineteen forty-three.
Strange craft flew above our head
with only one light winking red.
We had travelled back in time,
that's what the pilot said.
But this morning when I awoke
I had dreamt this whilst in bed.

S Glover

IT GHOSTS TO SHOW

A miser alone in a garret was counting his ill-gotten gold.
He'd murdered his wife for her money as now this grim story is told.
And as he sat counting the sovereigns ('twas a dark and tempestuous night),
He chewed at a crust for his supper and was lit by a candle's dim light.
He'd murdered his wife for her money, cut her head off so she couldn't talk,
To make sure she'd stay where he'd put her, cut her feet off so she couldn't walk.
The wind whistled loud through the shutters and rattled the latch on the door,
But what was that sound that he heard then above the storm's fierce blustery roar?
At first he just tried to ignore it and thought it was only a rat,
But the sounds came again only louder, slither bump, slither bump, pit-a-pat.
The sounds became nearer and nearer, slither bumping along up the stair,
Then the door of the garret flew open, oh what did he see standing there?
'Twas the ghost of his wife that he saw there, headless, footless and all robed in white,
And seeing she'd come back to haunt him, it gave him a terrible fright.
He jumped into his bed and lay trembling and pulled the sheet over his head,
He heard the ghost come slithering nearer, till it stopped at the foot of the bed.
And what happened next, did she kill him? The end of this story ensures
That she lifted the sheet and pulled hard on his leg,
Just the same as I'm pulling on yours!

Margaret B Baguley

ALL THEIR PLANS DISPERSED

Her suitcases packed, were placed side by side, in the dark hall,
She quickly applied another make-up layer to her face.
Knowing it's over, would be hardly any time at all,
Until she had escaped from this extremely dreary place.

Wooden hairbrush in hand, long gentle downward strokes she gave,
She looked towards the window but could not see his blue car.
In the mirror her face returned a steady prolonged gaze,
Knew he was driving, collecting her, he could not be far.

She surveyed the enormous pink bedroom for the last time,
It appeared that all was going exactly to her plan.
And she thought this old house never really did feel like mine,
Then, outside in the lane, she heard a ominous bang.

Suddenly, all of her ideas, her schemes, had all dispersed,
While smoke and flames from her lover's car filled the morning sky.
In the lane, juggernaut lorry into car had reversed,
Before she could get to him she was certain he would die.

S Mullinger

THE PERFORMER

He took great care with his debut
And the critics gave a rare review.
Some said 'Just right for the part.'
Others wrote, 'An excellent start.'

Was he on his way to fame?
To have lights put round his name?
Theatre can be so precarious
Dramatic - or just hilarious.

Audiences are what thespians crave
And for their art they are willing to slave.
Auditions and parts may be few
But some are exactly right for you.

So when you get the chance to shine,
No matter if it's pantomime.
For every dog may have his day
But cats purr-form a special way.

Our Tom can definitely vouch for that,
Dick Whittington's nothing without his cat!

H D Hensman

SHOPPING

I'm stood outside a superstore awaiting the stampede,
It's nearly time to unlock door, the first is knobbly-kneed.
She's moaning that we're in a line and joined in a tight clench,
Of all the trolleys, she wants mine, she's won - but what a wrench!
We're in, determined no delay, I think I'll have some fun
And point myself a different way so she can bump someone.
It's my friend with the wonky wheel, we've started quite a row,
I've really grazed the sandalled heel of skinny legs - and how!
She's moaning that they've changed the shelves and checking
                                                    sell-by day,
I think, while at the back she delves, I'll travel on my way.
I'm passing one that has a chair, it's carrying a child
With ice cream running everywhere, now that would make me wild.
I see my mate is in the wars with hairy legs to thank
He's aiming wide perhaps because he used to drive a tank.
The miniskirt knows she's the star, male audience to please,
She doesn't need to bend that far to pick up frozen peas!
At last we've passed the checkout stand, I don't want her again,
She's left me in the car park and it's pouring down with rain.
A Nora Batty wrinkly one with a soaking brolly
Is pushing me at everyone - who'd be a shopping trolley!

Pam Owers

DISCOVERY

As we sweated under a burning sun
Sifting and brushing over sand and stone
The archaeological dig had taken shape
On our hands and knees we chipped away
Suddenly the ground just opened up
And into the unknown fell the three of us

Bruised and shaken from head to toe
In a cloud of dust we coughed and choked
Then came a high-pitched screeching sound
And the demon with a thousand eyes came down
We huddled close, numb with fright
As the bats flew over and out of sight

Lost in this shadowland of catacombs
We all knew this could be our tomb
Then our eyes feasted on a magical place
As we came across the most enormous cave
There were drawings from the dawn of time
With dinosaurs and caveman life
As we shuffled along we came to the last
We saw the bug-eyed aliens - and their giant spacecraft . . .

Frank Howarth-Hynes

KNOWING ONE'S PLACE

We drove in through the gilded gates,
Passed the South Lodge and down along
The blazing rhododendron drive
Missing an odd pheasant or two,
Parked below the Ha-Ha on the
Field with the panoramic views.

We stood where once we dared not stand
Our humble two pounds paid to boost
The funds of some fine charity,
Peered in through half-drawn curtains
Glimpsed chandeliers sparkling bright
And giant bowls of flowers, blue.

We idled around the fountain
Built to celebrate some great day
Gaped at wide herbaceous borders
Yards and yards in length, on towards
The lake, the bog and walled gardens
And places housing toothsome fruits.

Brazenly sat on garden seats
Owned by some great lord or other,
Touched the plants and smelt the orchids
Taking up at last the offer
A home-baked tea, not in the house
But in the stable yard, of course!

Myra Bowen

STOOD UP BY MY UMBRELLA

We're not like other people,
With an umbrella stand.
Or a place to place
Your walking stick,
When you don't need it at hand.
Why is it when it's raining
You cannot find the spot,
The place your umbrella was,
Your umbrella's not?
You look into the stair cupboard,
Into every single drawer.
You even check the garage,
And open the car door.
Why is it when it's raining
You find that at your cost,
Someone's taken your umbrella,
Or at worst it's just got lost
You dash about for hours
Trying to find what's just not there.
So when you step out of the door,
You do not wet your hair.
You fumble here, you fumble there.
You think that you've been cursed,
Because when you step out of the door
The clouds begin to burst.
You dash down to the local shop
To buy a loaf of bread.
You've got yourself soaked to the skin
Your hair's stuck to your head.
Then just as you are leaving,
From the puddle in the shop,
And you're shivering and sneezing,
The checkout girl shouts, 'Stop!'
You turn around, you stop and stare.

You don't know what to say,
Because the checkout girl she found it
At the checkout yesterday.
You know it's just not funny
As you step out of the door,
Because the weather's just turned sunny,
And you just can take much more.

Charles David Jenkins

WHERE'S THE TOWN CENTRE?

You cannot find Great Witley.
You search with all your might.
It came out in the open once
then dodged back out of sight.

The roads go racing past it.
The signposts are at odds . . .
And don't go asking people
they're a funny lot of sods.

Nearby they have this famous church
where spirits whinge and whine.
They thought they'd reached Great Witley
but they'd never crossed the line.

Then there's this place called Witley Court.
The grass once overrun it.
It cost a bomb, went up in smoke,
And nob'dy knows who done it!

I think this place, Great Witley,
is houses that were spilt
by all surrounding neighbours
on a town they never built . . .

but there are those with hearts of oak
inside each cottage gate,
etched into England's countryside
to make Great Witley great,

so use your mind, and force your heart,
to fashion compositely
a Camelot from times forgot . . .
and then you've got: Great Witley.

Leonard Jeffries.

TEMPTATION

I had been looking forward to this liaison a whole week,
Temptation, one might say,
Yes, I have succumbed before,
It has to be said, I am weak,
Yet those little words that greet me are very significant,
I have received other offers of course,
But could not oblige them all,
For me it has to be something really special,
And as I make my way to the chosen destination,
Thoughts drift through my mind,

My heart starts to beat faster,
Soon my every desire will be filled,
Just as on so many occasions of late,
On arrival, I tentatively look around,
Waiting for that special moment,
That brief encounter,
Whilst trying not to look too interested,
Familiarity breeds contempt and all that,
I ponder on the past when my life had been mundane,
And to the present which offers so much,

A shopping trolley brims with sumptuous goodies,
Carefully placed onto the conveyor belt,
The checkout operator scans intently,
Whilst the store manager stands smiling with satisfaction,
My husband's wallet bare, apart from moths,
I had sauntered up every aisle,
Searched and perused every sign,
Grabbed every bargain available,
Two for the price of one, buy two get one free,
Freebies, the housewife's dream come true.

Ann G Wallace

THE ONE THAT GOT AWAY

Sitting in the launderette, 2 by 3 on a seat
This has got to be the looked-for weekly treat!
Watching the clothes go round and around
Mesmerised and bombarded by the washtub sound.

The laundry begins to dance, but starts off rather slow
Waiting for its partner who then begins to flow.
Working up speed after a dignified gavotte
Intermingling real crazy till it's hard to know what's what!

A tortured sock looks out, a blue and crumpled face,
Replaced almost immediately by a white one in lace.
Tangled and damp, skirt follows sheet,
Until all is ready for the basket posed on seat.

Eating up the money, the heater then is next,
Coin after coin, it's something to make one vexed,
The revolution continues but eventually comes to a halt
And out comes a shirt with a tremendous vault.

Some time now has passed, so we must in haste leave,
Having filled the adjacent bag with a last almighty heave.
We sort out everything at home, sweaters, clothes and frock
Oh no, just don't believe it, we are missing the blue sock!

Daphne McFadyen

I'M IN LOVE

I stand and I admire you
Your body is so sleek
I would give you anything
For just a moment's peek
The way you're dressed
It turns me on
Your leather makes me hot
I run my hands
All down your top
My God, I should be shot
A big smart guy
Walks up to me
And say you can't resist her
I reply with bated breath
I'll stick with my Fiesta!

M J Morgan

DARK BLACK COAT

He sits beside me in his dark black coat
As we journey through the moonlit land
His eyes watch my every move as I raise my left hand
My timepiece shows it's midnight clear
This the hour that brings its own fear.
I look up at the moon
The night air caresses my throat
As he sits beside me in his dark black coat

We hurtle along in this swaying coach
He licks his lips my heart turns cold
Oh how I wish we were not alone
I turn my head, he is quite close
His warm breath I feel against my throat
The coach stops
It's time to alight
Just before my dog takes his first bite.

Susan Lewis

BLACK NARCISSUS

It is cold at night
In the desert
As burning sun
Gives birth to freezing moon.
A man wanders aimlessly
Trying to make sense
Of the emptiness that surrounds him.

The desert is a good place
For self-discovery.

Much love he has spent
From a bankrupt heart.
Love that was freely given
But never returned.
Still he navigates this vast expanse
These oceans of sand
Shifting through gears of uncertainty.

In this waterless place
He thirsts for the truth.

He has walked many miles
Seen countless images of perfection,
All of them came to nothing
Vanishing as he drew near.
His blistering eyes
Blinded by the glare
Of an impossible dream.

At his feet a black narcissus
The symbol of mangled beauty.

Ian Barton

AT LAST YOU FOUND ME
(Dedicated to James Green)

The black clouds hid the sun
The rain descended all around.
It was like a bad storm at sea,
The wind whirled without a sound.

The ground was drowning
The rain was overcoming me,
It was beating down and down
The once dry land was now covering me.

No people around to help me
All alone once again
No light to guide me
Through this pouring rain.

The rain went on - never stopped
The rain was winning me.
All of a sudden the sun broke through
And warmth fell on my sea.

The sea disappeared along with every drop of rain
I could walk on the ground once again.
I no longer was alone, I had a friend
And because of you my pain is at its end.

Jodie McKane

WHO'S WHO?

A boy stood by an Indian,
Day had just begun,
The Indian was not his dad,
But the boy was the Indian's son.

The Indian was tall and proud,
And that was clear to see,
But it's their relationship,
That really puzzles me.

Then came along another boy,
He too was the Indian's son,
The Indian was not their dad,
The Indian was their mum.

John Napier Williams

THE STONE LION

The black iron-scrolled gates hang now on their sides,
and the ivy creeps through the cracks, in the earth, in the stone,
the lion statue's engraved words, that the moss now hides,
all that's left to explain why the house stands alone.

Broken glass reflects with a thousand edges,
all that remains of the windows now lifeless, now shattered,
wilderness, wilfully defying established hedges,
far removed from pristine, now merely tattered.

A door of dark wood still stands, formidably tall,
with a brass knocker, worn like a badge, like a star,
yet a crudely-nailed plank forbids entrance to all,
red bricks crumble and fall, while cracks spread far.

Few slates on the roof are left to keep out the cold,
rain invited in, splashes down the staircase, down the wall,
an echoed memory of music now faint, but once bold,
drifts into the past, lost, along the length of the hall.

The carved stone lion stands guard by the old gate,
a warning, don't pass through the gate, that is black-scrolled iron,
leave now the saddened house to its inevitable fate,
how foolish the owner who brought a cursed stone statue of a lion.

Caroline Ayre

THE BALANCE OF NATURE

The hyena is partial to the taste
of a half-eaten decomposed carcass
whilst the giraffe prefers the flavour
of the lofty acacia leaves.
Thus nature's equalities
are maintained by the fact
that the giraffe is a vegetarian
and that the hyena cannot climb trees.

The chauffeur, liveried in his car
has never tasted caviar
whilst in the back his master's lips
have never closed on fish and chips.

If the driver could scale the social heights;
if the noble could suffer the worst
contracting pains of an empty belly,
then the giraffe's legs would get shorter,
the hyena would acquire a longer neck
and the balance would have been reversed.

Barry Langley

PLAGUE

Not a cloven hoof
Between here and . . .

Hell!

But what of the fauns?

Have they too gone down choking,
In a welter of burning froth
Between the soft-eyed cattle
And a lifetime's winnowing?
Or had they gone before?

Perhaps the train's klaxon
Or the earlier whistles
Scared them into trees
And the trees have been cut down

No one has seen them
For a memory or more
But that is scarcely surprising
For even if they are around us still
And why should disease
Or trains affect them. . .?
And they breathed on
The glass walls of our names -
We would never notice,
Complain of vertigo
Or ask the doctor for another pill!

'. . . but my Dear
Isn't it awful?

Still, they are only animals
After all.
And the price of meat my Dear
Will drive us to the wall.'

Jeffrey A Pickford

CAPITALISM

I am as poor as a church mouse,
And as mean as muck,
So when you come to my house,
You will just have to take pot luck.

But beware as my mouth goes into gear,
Before warning bells in my brain,
So if you are found insincere,
I will respond with my tongue, without shame.

Although I am as poor as a church mouse,
And as mean as muck,
I am a vitriolic mistress of my house,
As the notice on my door warns. If you care to look.

I am short of nothing that I have got,
And as I've got nothing you are welcome to share,
For years *'friends'* who continued had a dreadful shock,
When it became abundantly clear my bank balance was bare.

Now being as poor as a church mouse,
And as mean as muck
Friends no longer visit my house,
There is nothing to gain, just plain pot luck.

Jay Baker

Rude Awakening

They came on a coach tour from England
But actually met in France
He knew he had found the perfect love
From that special very first glance

Holiday over, thought he'd give her a call
She lay in her garden with one leg agin' the wall
Her glass eye in a dish looking quite bland
Blonde wig arranged on a colourful stand

Dentures there also, his mind took a spin
She held out her hand, gave a toothless grin
He ran and he ran till he caught his train
Vowed never, oh never, to go there again!

He started to shake, his body aquiver
Sweat poured out just like a river
A pat on the shoulder, his dad, face agleam
'Here's a cup of tea lad, had a bad dream . . .?'

J Howling Smith

FRIENDS

I only came to tell you what I thought of you.
I only came to see what you were like.
I only came to you to vent my anger
Using words like, 'whore' and 'village bike'.

I didn't come prepared to find I liked you,
That we'd have so much in common, you and I
And I didn't come prepared that I would share you
With the man who brought a sparkle to my eye.

I didn't come prepared for what might happen
When a marriage of long-standing almost ends
Or that though you and my husband were once lovers
The two of us would stay the firmest friends.

Joyce Walker

DEJECTED

She sat before me
Holding onto my hand.
'I know that it's hard love
But I do understand.
It's like that with some men,
Or so I've been told.
It's nothing to do with age
Though you are getting old.
So don't feel dejected
And looking so downcast,
The sorrow that you feel now
I know it soon will pass.
And if you cannot do it,
Then so be it.
But to tell you the truth love,
You'll never learn to knit.

J A Silkstone

MYSTERY TRIP

The Head announced our pleasure trip would be
A memorable event of mystery,
The first in our school's ten-year history.
Outings were rare.

Wonder and disbelief on every face -
Excited notions darting place to place
Like frisky mountain breezes in a race
Going nowhere.

The day came. Waking thoughts aroused the thrill.
Leaping from bed despite the early chill
With port of call remaining secret still.
Not long to wait!

We met, in groups, with uncontrolled elation,
Laid bets (pennies) on likely destination
Then walked exuberantly onto the station.
No one was late!

The secret was well-kept - we had no clue
Of terminus arranged. Nobody knew!
Excitedly we waited in a queue -
As English do!

The air electric with anticipation
Erupted with antenna's information,
The train for Northgate's mystery location
To Thorpeness, is now entering the station.'
B R - Trust you!

Joy Saunders

THE PIXIE'S PARTY

The little 'Devon Pixie'
Held a party one fine night
He invited all the glow-worms
And the fireflies to give light

All the garden gnomes
And the fairies all went too
Their wings were brightly coloured
A beautiful rainbow hue

The mushrooms were the tables
Some mounds of grass the chairs
They drank the dew in buttercups
And feasted on some pears

The music was from the nightingales
And the crickets' whistling call
Everyone enjoyed it
They really had a ball

Some baby rabbits joined in the fun
And scampered round and round
Then everyone just disappeared
When I awoke there wasn't a sound.

Violetta J Ferguson

THE PERFECT PAIR

We two have been together
For many, many years.
Living in domestic harmony,
With no cross words or bitter tears.

We have worked for many different people,
Always to their satisfaction.
Never tired of being needed
Never causing hostile reaction.

Unhappy working as an individual,
Ever dedicated as a team.
All for one and one for all,
All our kind are just as keen.

Though some would treat us roughly,
Then we go in terror of our lives.
Our enemies, the fathers and their children,
The kind and gentle ones, the wives.

Never wanting to be parted.
To you, we seem no better than we oughter!
So, when all is said and done dear friends
We are only a cup and saucer!

Molly M Hamilton

EPITAPHS

Here lies my body broken asunder
Six feet long and six feet under
Frozen stiff and slightly perished
But elixir itself to the worm it's nourished.

I am risen now I have ascended
I'm at that place where you go when you die
I climbed on such an uplifting thermal
Convection in the eternal sky.

And here in this my burial place
Me and the Almighty are face to face
And yet I cannot think it right
God incarnate as a tiny mite.

I'm pleased to report that I've met the Redeemer
Relax below, all you that have sinned
Just look to the plume and you'll see me there
Forgiven and blown by the wind.

Here lies my body and this is where I'm
Settling down nicely at the end of my time
Six feet below and madly in love
With sweet little Daisy who's six feet above.

But there are one or two things that I must address
Before you bury or burn and lay me to rest,
Can I have a nice send-off with lovely white flowers
And hymns and kind words that go on for hours?

Jack Bowden

PIE IN THE SKY

She sat beside me on the bed
'Please! Give it to me now,' she said

And meant it

Then with a twinkle in her eye
'Come on' she said, 'now don't be shy'

I want it

She cuddled up to a degree
And in a while was squeezing me

I liked it

Just as my heart began to pound
She raised her arm without a sound

I said . . . 'Hold it!'

She paid no heed to my demand
And snatched the mince pie from my hand

And ate it.

Maurice Ivor Birch

A Schoolboy's Dream

So beautiful, so like a dream,
Beckoning, lying in the grass.
Soft tanned skin, like darkened cream,
So tempting that he could not pass.

He knelt, caressed with hand
The rounded shape so smooth.
Never saw a sight so grand,
Decided then to make his move.

Lovingly said last goodbye,
He could not keep this lovely one,
Touched with lips, then with a sigh,
Thrust deep, alas was done.

He quickly threaded on the string,
Then held his prize up high.
Then suddenly with fearful swing,
He saw his mighty conker die.

Harry Gill

Encounter

He stood still, watching her silently -
A girl of some nine summers
Sitting beneath the larch tree, reading.
This was his land, private land,
There should be no trespassing he thought,
She has no right to be there.
But then he remembered a small boy
Running to the same old tree,
Shouts of anger ringing in his ears
Till he reached his secret place
To miss an unjust beating.
The child looked up, smiled at him,
Saw an old man stern-faced, stick in hand
Walking towards her slowly.
'When you want to hide,' he said, 'come here
It can be your special tree.'
Now she is older than he was then
And smiles as she remembers.
'How are we today dear?' says the nurse
Rearranging the pillows.
I don't know about you, thinks her brain
I'm reading under the larch tree.

Patricia M Ponting

HAZARD OF OZ

Give back my cousin, rogues of Oz, you scoundrels Down Under
returned to us after long, long years, I wonder
where is the shy girl that we knew so well
so quiet, so petite on departing these shores
returned but briefly, who's this handmaid from Hell

Dive under the seat, dig deep in the hole, chasing coney
as she loudly berates the driver over money
I'm not buying your bus, you conning preacher
this from a youngster who played hooky from school
oh! So afraid of a teacher

Goblin shakes on his rafters, windows bend to the snores
the Gnome in his cellar fills cracks in the floors
this vast whale on the bed cares not noon is near
if this is my cousin I must love her still
yet even the hearth cricket departed in fear

She pecked with sparrows round the small dinner platter
they've finished and gone, but her time did not matter
now the mice are starving, behind the fridge, the lurcher's
                                              growing thinner
full plates are emptied down a cavernous throat
while even the broomstick's waxing slimmer

The Ogre in the well drank us dry and absconded
the Trolls sank the privy, fathoms deep, and it's foundered
our oven's erratic, we have rock-hard bread
but these things happen, it can't be all bad
see, most of our mail looks pretty in red

Take back my cousin, good cobbers of Oz, fair diggers of Perth
I've many fine thoughts of you, far side of this earth
she's a gorgeous person, I do love her so fine
but I'd treasure her so much more, I'm sure
at the far distant end of a telephone line

Erchin Diss

THE HAPPY WANDERER

I had a thought - could I leave the comforts of my home?
How I'd like to be a wanderer the countryside to roam
Put on my boots woolly hat a rucksack on my back.
Oh! I must remember a brolly and a mac!
I'll travel light with few essentials - a cup - a plate, a spoon.
How exciting to eat supper by the light of the moon!
To watch little lambs and rabbits hear the birdies sing
Fresh air and simple pleasures that Nature will bring
'Oh to be in England now that spring is here'
I'll have a stroll in the woods might even see some deer.
At night I'll sleep in a cosy barn
Early morning splash my face in a tarn
Adventurous, exciting this would all seem
Unfortunately it's all in a dream!
To rough it outside I'm not that kind
These are fancies all in my mind
I love warmth and comfort to sleep in my bed
Have you guessed? It's all in my head!

Ethel Wakeford

AN EARLY DATE

You hesitate
When the stream's in spate
Even though you're late0
For that early date.
Which would she berate?
A late date or a soaking reprobate
You can hardly wait
To confirm your fate.

So you plunge on in and levitate
To the distant shore where you celebrate
Certain now she will appreciate
Your every attempt to participate
In that early date.

But . . . your wet, soggy boots just infuriate
Your sticky, wet jeans do not titillate
It seems you are certain to saturate
The special dress bought to captivate,
The tongue lashes on till you extricate
Your battered, wet soul to recuperate
At home, where you ruminate
That the very next time the stream's in spate
Don't hesitate
Turn around, let her wait
Or emigrate
At an early date.

J Aldred

THE GIFT

Always on the frail side,
A very scrawny child!
Going at my own pace,
Which was never wild.

Often, I got left behind,
In games, requiring speed,
And when it came to teams,
Me, they did not heed!

Then one day, my life changed,
A birthday gift! For me?
From neighbours in our street,
My eyes lit up with glee!

I did all their shopping,
Took babies for a walk,
Babysat their children,
Read to them, or we'd just talk.

It was no chore, I loved it,
and didn't realise,
It was any 'big deal,'
That gift was some surprise.

Freedom now was mine!
For, when friends went on a a hike,
Instead of puffing laboriously,
I kept up! On my new *bike!*

E M Eagle

THE MOUSE

The grey, featureless mouse is condemned
To live alone,
An outcast from the nest.
The hard, hand-held body
Is greatly swollen through evolution.
Inside the hollow abdomen,
The implant of modern technology breathes life
Into the stone-still thalidomide form.
The informant hand pilots the blind mouse
- The pointer of information -
Intelligently gliding on the underbelly's small, domed rubber ball.
The steady hand continuously feeds the featureless mouse.

Louise Mills

I CAN BE

I am a friend
who reaches out to another.
A daughter who is loved
and cared about.

But the roles can be reversed.
I can be a friend that listens,
while another reaches out.
A daughter who is not noticed.
A sister that is a companion.

How about a brother
who tells the sister out of love
or a brother who is a friend?

And a father who shares his love
amongst his children?

I might be a mother,
who brings new meaning
to the word life.

Ise Obomhense

COPRESENCE

Baseless allegations of a flying metal disc
A new and original light on events
Soaring, leaving the ocean behind
Is a psychic shock unbounded
For the tea-sipping passengers on the cruise past Heligoland.

Michael C Soper

HARLEY STREET

'Doctor, why do you always ask the patients what they eat,
No matter what the problem, from the head down to their feet?
Does it have a bearing upon the therapy?'
'Oh no, it's a handy guide to what I can charge, you see.'

G H Bryant

OUR LASTING ROSES

Thorns no longer catch those sheets on high lines,
Your perfume such a delicate fragrance, sweetening the air,
Once saw us all play as children just there . . .

We made scents from your petals, then sold them . . .
Pretend games the same . . . your eyes watched us then
Through our garden wall. You spread out deep roots
And smiled at us all.

Lesley J Worrall

A Time To Play

There is a little girl round here
Who likes to play the piano.
She practises it all times of day
And has a don't care manner.
But sometimes the girl will trust the words
And the boys are just as bad.
I'm just so very glad, I love the boys I have,
I like to see the children play on a summer's day.
I will pull the curtain back again,
So I can see them play.
They often give me a little wave.
That gives me a little thrill
And helps me feel quite good.
They marked the ground with chalk and stones
To play their games today.
Not many children go to play,
The TV stops all that.
The computer and the games are fun,
They prefer it to a chat.
The art of talking now is almost gone,
No one has time to chat.

Heather Breadnam

LOST MY MIND

Lost my mind, don't know where,
Didn't know it was missing,
Until I found it wasn't there.
Lost my keys, locked in my mind.
Lost my wallet, bank cards I can't find.
Lost my teeth, don't know what to say.
Lost my comb, haven't lost my hair.

Lost the feeling in my arm,
When I shoved it down the chair.
Found a fifty pence piece,
Didn't know was there.
Checked my pockets, found a hole.
How did that get there?
At least I've found one of my legs,
I hope, one of a pair.

Now if I hadn't lost my mind,
I'd find those things I can't find.
I'll look inside her handbag
While she's not around,
It's a treasure chest, a magpie's nest,
Of everything no one collects.
There are paper clips, half-eaten crisps,
A million bus tickets of nowhere trips.
Used handkerchiefs, elastic bands,
Another batch of final demands.
Ouch! I found a needle.
Who put that in there?
Now isn't that typical,
I find the needle in the haystack,
But the haystack isn't there.

Charles David Jenkins

GUESS WHO

Everyone has got one
But do we really care?
If we were to lose it,
Would we even shed a hair?

Would you both like to be parted?
I doubt it, it is nice,
If you had to go without it,
I'm sure you'd think about it twice.

It's like a second nature,
It's company in a way,
Remember when as children
It was fun to have a play.

It's nice to take it with you
On a really sunny day,
And when the sun is setting
You can watch it slip away.

Have you guessed who our old friend is,
Who is really like a ghost?
Why, it's our very own dear shadow
And the one we love the most.

Yes, we all have got one,
It's not difficult to find,
Just glance over your shoulder,
Or take a look behind.

Joyce Hammond

ALMOST ONE OF THE FAMILY

The moment the car
Turned into the road,
She went to visit a friend.
To me it was the end.
The final straw.
After all, he was almost
One of the family.
And you have to play host
Or in our case hostess
To a guest.

It was bad enough
Before Christmas
That sharp exchange
Beside the tree.
Sister shot upstairs
Refusing to come down for tea,
And he sat with an inscrutable look
Till the family took their leave.
I could not believe
Her persistent disdain.
I've pointed out again and again,
You have to get on with relations.
She replied with a toss of her head
'Cousins perhaps, but dog and cat
Were not meant to be friends
And that's that!'

Freda Grieve

BEDTIME SOUNDS

Loud angry voices ring out
Echoing like bursts of thunder
Hard blows fly as lightning
Flashing across the night sky
We cling to each other, our pillows
Wet from falling tears
We lay almost motionless
In our small bed
Waiting for the storm to pass by
In their arguments and bitterness
They forget the vulnerable little ones
Who once they made in love to one another.

Deborah Grimwade

I AM BEAUTIFUL

I am beautiful,
People travel from afar to look at me,
When sometimes I lay bare they do not sight see,
Loving me for what I am, their chickadee.

I often dress in resplendent radiance,
My main aim being to attract an audience,
A regal sight to behold,
I'm known for wearing masses of gold.

Artists find me irresistible,
Poets enjoyable,
All find me approachable,
Just occasionally impossible, being impassable.

If I am neglected
I become dejected,
Run wild in disarray,
Looking attractive, at my best, my metier.

Constant attention is my goal, unashamedly,
Many spend their lives with me,
To show appreciation and glee,
I blossom and bloom thro' the year, profusely,
Me boast? I beg your pardon
I am an exquisite garden!

Hilary Jill Robson

SNOWFLAKES

She watches as flaked rain dances provocatively
in the halogen glow of the street light.

Each of us a single crystal,
momentarily free, falling alone.

Small,
Powerless.

Until each becomes a thread
in a thickly woven blanket.

This new scene looks pure,
tactile and alluring,
Picture postcard pretty of adorning virgin snow.

Relentlessly we invade every nook and cranny,
Stealthy our drifts catch man unawares,
his machines admit defeat.

The now white world
Shudders to a silent halt.

The gritters and ploughs
forge on through barricaded roads
but they are never a threat to our whole.

Children like us,
they can fight and play,
growing rosy-cheeked
and healthy.

She watches smiling,
For what is there to fear?

A single snowflake
cannot kill.

Jean Caldwell

TUBE LINE

Crying in the subway, carrier bags strewn around,
No shining knight in armour, toothless wizened
weirdo shuffled into view, trousers bagged around the ankles,
clutched in front, without even the usual piece of string,
clothes encrusted with careless wear of ages old,
clean skin but food in stubbed chin.
A person hobbled into dance and nasaled into sing
and cheered my lonely self absorb, made me feel
a little different.
When I gave him money (widow's mite sized, all there was)
he was embarrassed and insisted on following me
all the way down the line, explaining his own story,
murders he'd been witness to, milkman's jokes from yester age,
relatives in hospital, how he thought I was a bag lady
and definitely needed cheering up.

Lesley Vann

My Bike

I once had a bike it was yellow
with transfers all sparkling and new,
I raced it a lot, so the tyres were shot
and the brakes were completely worn through.

I loved my bike it was a pal of mine
I had loved it for quite some years
I sold it to the bloke who lived next door
It brought me so near to tears.

I watched him ride it many times and
thought that should be me, and I thought
back to those many times I had ridden it by
the sea, it was a racer beyond a doubt
with down-turned handles that stuck out.

With a light-weight frame and a seat so slim
that brought tears to my eyes while I broke
it in. The seat was all shiny and black
and I polished it till I couldn't tether
the seat was so hard till it softened with lard
one could not tell it was leather.
My bike, my pal.

Francis Joseph Lawton

STAY WITH ME

'Stay with me,' it whispered
'Don't leave me on my own.
I'm lonely and it's quiet
When you're away from home.'

'I have to go, I cannot stay
I have a job to do,
Don't be sad and don't be lonely
For you know that I love you.

On my return we'll have a cuddle
and I'll sink into your arms
I'll feel your strength and comfort
And enjoy all of your charms.

But now I have to leave you
To feel the wind blow through my hair
But I will be thinking of you
My green reclining chair!'

Linda Cooper

WHO KILLED MY BROTHER?

Who killed my kin,
Left him hanging out to die?
Was he killed by a djinn,
A spirit from the sky?

His body was entombed in a casket,
Wrapped tightly in silken thread.
His body hung up on a parapet,
By a person by whom he was misled.

A figure emerged from the darkness,
Moving slowly on a tightrope of silken thread.
'Are you asking or telling, my pretty thing?'
'Asking,' replied the voice filled with dread.

'Then it was I,' said the spider to the fly.
'I killed your brother, and now you're going to die.'

Andrew Brian Zipfell

THE CALL

The phone call
Day and night
Is it my loved one that's in sight?
No just a person
Who never speaks
Then all of a sudden squeaks

Constantly always there
Like a lion
In his lair
The phone call
Day and night
Suddenly stops without a fight

'How long?' I dare to ask
As I go about
Getting on with the task
Then the phone begins to ring
Only day and never night
Now isn't that a thing?

Kristina Howells

BEANS FOR SUPPER

A bunch of carrots wet,
    shrivelled like a slimy snail
A lettuce leaf looking wan
    and pale.
Two swollen sausages on a china plate
Some pâté past its sell-by date.

A strong smell of garlic from a
    defrosted pack
One onion sprouting right through
    its sack
A chunk of cheese with a
    pea-green rind
A pickled onion that has
    fallen behind.

Some rashers of bacon curled up
    to the sky
The sad remains of a
    chicken pie
Even the milk is missing its top
And that poor jelly - what a flop.

Thank goodness tomorrow is
    shopping day
All I can do is throw this
    lot away.
A good bottle of wine that's
    a must
I'll make some toast and cut off
    the crust!

Gloria Hargreaves

THE LAST DANCE

Throughout the course of this night her eyes have met mine
for the thousandth time.
I keep getting tongue-tied fluffing up my chat up lines.
I mean do I look alright are my clothes giving off the right impression.
My friends tell me I'm the life and soul of the party!
Oh no I've hesitated yet again!
I'll have another beer my old mate Dutch it'll be next time have no fear
She's blonde, blue-eyed, a perfect bust, curvaceous figure
                                            long lovely legs
Oh she's a must.
She dresses in designer clothes a posh accent she's slightly upper crust.
She's turned a few fellas down flat now how about that?
It looks as though I'm still in with a chance!
I hope they play a slow one for the last dance!
Two hours have gone by I must pluck up the courage I feel
                                            like I could cry!
She's a perfect vision to behold get yourself over there I'm told.
She's still looking I feel so embarrassed I feel ten years old
Just like a little boy wringing my hands in frustration why oh why?
So I finally walk over all big and bold.
She glances at me very seductively.
Well this is it finally we're together dancing cheek to cheek
I've been dying for this all week!
She runs her fingers through my hair phew I'm getting all excited
                                            down there.
She smiles promisingly at me she whispers in my ear
Ahh my greatest fear she's fourteen
I feel like a dirty old man!
I'm gutted I could scream it's so unfair it's bloody obscene!
The end of my night of passion with my angel my dream.

Jonathan Covington

MY LIFE WITHOUT YOU

I have to start a new beginning to put away the past,
Take the first step into something new,
I must be strong and true.
I miss you so very much my heart is aching,
My mind is numb, the sadness and yearning will fade with time,
The universe has spoken so we must succumb.
Maybe this will turn out to be a blessing in disguise,
For we will no longer have to battle for our emotions,
For our personal space, for our love and for understanding.

Maybe now we can be true comrades if we put aside our history,
While keeping the love inside we will give each other strength,
To carry us on through life,
I find it hard to keep you out of my thoughts,
We have been entwined for many years,
We have shared a magnitude of moments,
All of which must now be treasured memories,
Of a time when my life was with you.

I didn't know that you would turn my world inside out,
Upside-down no, life was never dull,
For you opened my eyes to so many things,
Yet everything's changing in our worlds,
Our paths now go different ways,
I know you will fare well on your way to transcendent.

For your power is strong,
We have not lost but have gained a friendship so strong,
For we are in each other's hearts and souls,
Nothing can ever change that my love.

Helen Legg

THE SILENT ARMY

Silently standing in long serried ranks
They have no need of weapons or tanks
To create confusion, and mild despair,
In the hearts of all who see them there.

Silently standing in red and white,
They have no need to move or fight.
Sometimes we wonder why they are there
But to move them away no one would dare.

Silently standing way into the distance,
They wouldn't offer any resistance.
Some get knocked over, and lie where they fall.
Nobody goes to their aid at all.

Silently standing for hour after hour,
Not doing anything, yet wielding such power.
Causing delays and moans and groans.
This silent army of motorway cones!

Jean M Wood

NINETEEN

He rebukes himself for thinking
he looks normal.
Over coffee he tries to steer
the conversation to the past
and watches the light behind his eyes
begin to fade away.

From the back of a wardrobe,
he reaches for his shoe box
laden with dust and heavy with demons.
He recalls the names of those
who didn't make it home -
who lie buried in swamp land,
jungle, darkness of ocean bed.

At last, the devils are released -
countless yellowing lines,
ribbons of rhymes,
fragments of still vivid odes.
Rhyming couplets consigned to memory,
now mouthed silently
through the tears;
stanzas stolen from forgotten moments,
similes as subtle as the passing of time.

Raising his eyes from the contents
spilling across his lap,
he comments how, in those days,
the average age of the poet
was nineteen.

Andrew Detheridge

THE DARK HORSE

She worked like hell.
It kept them fed.
It was a fact.
She left, just died.
It was a fact.

She left her lot.
They felt slightly cheated.
Could be lots more.
On seeing some numbers.
Could this be money?

Looked like bank number.
They checked it out.
Telephone number it was.
Dialled it turned out.

Mother had a lover.
The loyal old workhorse.
Had the last laugh.
'Wasn't she the dark horse?'

Margaret Gleeson Spanos

SPINSTER'S SONG

With men I've not had much success
I'm getting on, I must confess.
I paint my face and perm my hair
And pray some fellow waits out there.
My widowed ma will nag and scold
To be a grandma 'fore she's old.
All my friends and close relations
Yearn for wedding invitations,
Hints are dropped bold and unsubtle
Impossible to make rebuttal.
All hope had fled, until one day
My friend's third cousin came to stay.
He wasn't much to look at mind
But welcomed me - a date quite blind.
Things progressed, I hoped anew,
My parent make him tasty stew
She welcomed him with open arms
And complimented on his charms.
At last I wasn't county mouse
I had a man about the house.
'Twas not to be, I lost my lover
He jilted me and married Mother!

Sarah Blackmore

MOVING HOUSE MADNESS

I was trying to move house today
But everything got in my way,
Those trying to help
Made me yelp
When they threw my best clothes away.

Lindsey Brown

A FENCE TOO FAR

I had a horse and called him Shaz
A beautiful Arabian stallion
My boss decided to show him off
And win himself a medallion
To win he had to jump a fence
Though small 'twas two feet high
I galloped up to take the jump
But he simply wouldn't try
So drastic steps we had to take
I was told to hang on tight
My boss he hid behind the bush
Then rushed with all his might
He chased my horse and prodded him
With a prodder with such a sting
He caught him in an awkward place
And oh how he did fling
He bucked and kicked and cleared the jump
And several more besides
He threw me off and raced around
With water in his eyes
Soon back on top we tried again
And Shaz jumped all the poles
So home we went with confidence
We now could win our goals
The next day came and in the ring
A grand performance done
I aimed him for the two feet jump
He stopped and wouldn't run
Over I went without my horse
I was left there in the brink
I sank in water to my neck
And my horse began to drink.

Catherine Armstrong

TEA WITHOUT

She was only a girl in a tea shop
And he a bearded patrician,
But they looked at each other
With love and delight
And bother their social position!

She was only a girl in a tea shop
With intellect nothing at all,
But she knew how to woo
As most women do
And that is no mean thing at all!

She was only a girl in a tea shop
But she knew how to brew a strong draught,
She brewed her bold way
To his heart so they say
She certainly wasn't so daft!

She was only a girl in a tea shop
But she cut currant bread with a dash,
She sliced half her way
Through his fortune they say
Old fool now, without any cash!

The moral is there: now men be aware
If into a tea shop you go,
Show no concern
For the girl with the urn
Or your riches may suddenly flow!

Graham K A Walker

A Sense Of Humour

If you see the funny side
You'll stroll along the sunny side
Things will never harass you
Embitter or embarrass you
A sense of humour is the finest aid.

To wisdom in trouble and adversity
It brings you smiling through the stress
To cultivate the power to see
The little touch of comedy
Behind the tragedies of life.

D A Sheasby

THAT CERTAIN AGE

I'm at a certain age in life
    when I really do not care,
when politics disgusts me
    and comfort clothes I wear.

I'm weary of my aching back
    of rubbing cream and oils,
I sometimes doubt if man was made
    to be upright in his toils.

I wish I could be like the rest
    live retirement sort of lazy,
instead I'm writing poetry
    which proves I must be crazy.

And how I feel my ageing self
    quite often cross and grumpy,
I'll bet you when I'm in my box
    the coffin will be lumpy.

Then down below in Satan's Hell
    the Devil, he will greet me,
I'll swear at him right to his face
    if he bullies or ill-treats me.

He'll soon get tired of my complaints
    then ask God for a transfer.
God who knows me very well
    will just refuse to answer.

So back to Earth I shall return
    and haunt Westminster steeple,
I'll put my head beneath my arm
    and scare those wretched people.

Leslie Holgate

JUMPED OFF

There was an old lady called Mo,
Who really needed to let go.
Went behind a hedge for a pee,
In her knickers found a big flea.
Chasing it caused her a lot of strain,
It jumped into the grass and was never seen again.

Margaret Upson

LIMERICK

This is the story of Elsie Fudge,
Who when the train came
Refused to budge,
Now she's known as Elsie Sludge.

Alan Pow

HAY FEVER

A little boy had a runny nose
and every time he touched his toes
he had to give a hundred blows.

Of course it was in the PT class
and it was no joke - 'cos this pretty lass
she kept on kicking him on his 'ass'.

Every time she kicked his ass
mucus from his nose did pass -
it also made him want to wass.

And all because this pretty lass
who kept on kicking him on his ass
and every time he touched his toes
he had to give a hundred blows.

Now this little boy with the runny nose
who had to give a hundred blows
finished with a conk like a red, red rose.

By night he had a guiding light
but in the day he looked a sight
and looked as though he'd had a fight.

Now the girl who kicked him on his ass
really was a caring lass
and gently creamed his shiny nose
and promised whenever he touched his toes

She'd never ever kick him on his ass
and he was touched - said 'Be my lass.'

And now they're blessed with children three
each with a shiny nose like he
and every time they touch their toes
they have to give a hundred blows.

Mary Skelton

FUN

We went out to play in the snow,
And tried to have some fun
We laughed and played all day long
I fell and hurt my bum.

How we laughed,
I never will forget
Then after a while,
I found my pants were wet.

My hair was floppy
And in my face.
We still found time
To have a race.

Down the hill
In good style.
Then we all
Finished in a pile.

Tomorrow it's a brand new day,
Then again in the snow we'll play.

E Riggott

LADY FROM BUDE

A gallant young lady from Bude,
Who habitually slept in the nude,
Caught a burglar one night
And held on to him tight,
But the scene was, alas, misconstrued!

Molly Mettam

OFFICE POLITICS

The boss said, 'Someone is a traitor.
Just who is the tergiverstator?
My vital statistics
Are covered in lipstick!
Let's ask the administrator.'

That lady she had some aversion
To managers casting aspersions.
She said, 'It's ridiculous -
I'm always meticulous!
Perhaps it could be your perversion!'

The young secretary was next.
He sat frowning, appearing perplexed.
Said,' Who can it be?
It was probably me.
Please punish me or I'll be vexed!'

Said another, 'It couldnae be him.
I suggest you look to your sen.
Well och aye the noo,
it was probably you!
You used your lipstick as a pen!'

Well the boss, she at least had the grace
To step back, looking slightly shamefaced
And send with a flick
The offending lipstick
Rolling into the bin in disgrace!

Anna Gillions

MORE ADVENTURES WITH SANTA CLAUS

Santa rides on his sleigh, singing his jolly 'Ho, ho'
Speeding with his reindeers, upon the jolly snow
They travel way out of Wonderland, bringing all the toys
And lots of little goodies, for little girls and boys

Now, Santa wears his glasses, and thinks he's jolly smart
If we wait a little longer, his adventures will jolly start
He tells the reindeers to run fast, which isn't so surprising
They run even more the faster, which isn't jolly amusing

A go slow notice is written, for bumps, are on the ground
Santa sees no notice, as a few toys drop around
He jerks along the roadside, on the snow he jelly slides
The reindeers look behind them, ears prop back, and to the sides

Santa picks up the little toys, to dry them with his cloak
What will he get up to next? Some kind of jolly joke
He ends up in a car park, and thinks it is jolly funny
A ticket collector sees him, and asks him for his money

The collector refuses to let him pass, until he pays the pound
Snow is still in Santa's ears, he doesn't hear a sound
'Do you know who I am?' says Santa upon this frosty night
'I don't care who you are,' he replies, ' you look a jolly sight'

Santa eventually climbs the chimney and gets stuck half the way
The soot has made him turn black, as it wasn't swept away
So sleep tight little children, do not go out to see
He will manage somehow, when he gets down the chimney

The reindeers have had enough, and are impatient to get back to
    Wonderland
So keep dreaming of the goodies, while you sleep in Slumber Land
Santa has gone, ringing the bells, 'Ho, ho' with jolly sounds of cheer
Hoping he will be full of fun, with more adventures next year

Jean P Edwards McGovern

WRAPPING PRESENTS

I started at the corner it's as easy
and daring you see.
Fold it down, sticky tape at the ready
I am happy as can be.
Fingers grasping, it's oh! Such a mess
Oh heck, now I need a rest
Oh, bottles all shapes and sizes it's no wonder
there is dizziness before my eyes
Noisy toys are deafness to me.
I shall need my headache pills at three.
Why do presents have to get so much bigger?
At this rate I won't get my dinner.
I have to do this when the boys are out
else all they will do is drum and shout
There now, that's the last, oh how happy!
My hour has past.

A J Renyard

JUNGLE TALES

Two fat ladies sat in a tree
whilst a lion prowled below expectantly.
Said Clarissa, 'This fungi looks just right.
We'll cook it with garlic and veal tonight.'

The branch gave way and, with a splat,
they fell and squashed the waiting cat.
'Phew, that was close,' said Clara with a shrug
'Thank goodness we fell on this old rug.'

'My thoughts exactly,' Clarissa did declare,
carelessly brushing a cobra from her hair.
'I know,' said Clara as the serpent fell.
'Let's go through a river, we can both swim well.'

So Clarissa and Clara swam through the Nile,
knocking out a rhino and a crocodile.
'That was good,' said Clara, shaking drops all over,
as ten elephants and a giraffe ran for cover.

'Bit disappointing,' said Clarissa as they reached campsite,
'That there were no animals out tonight.'

Linda Ann Johnson

OUR DOG

Our dog has a problem,
No stop it, don't laugh,

It's not funny really,
Don't stare as you pass,

But if he is searching
To look for his bone,

Or roaming the hillside
To find his way home,

Or sniffing out rabbits
From under the hedge,

Or chasing the birds
From our window ledge,

Or barking at cats
In the garden at night,

Or chasing the postman
Who gave him a fright,

Or if there's a she dog
That smiles as she passes,

To do all these things
Our dog has to wear glasses.

Jim Sargant

BABY SISTER

I love my baby sister, she really makes me laugh -
When she spins round and round in circles, and falls on her ***!
She's getting into everything, she won't stay still -
She climbs on the sofa and on the window sill
It's like fighting with an octopus when you change her nappy
And when you've finally finished, *she starts being happy!*
She tries to say words which don't come out quite right
And we're still trying to figure out what she means by 'ite'!
She likes reading books but chewing them is best,
The amount of cardboard in her belly is showing through her vest!
She's got a lovely smile and she can be really sweet,
Especially when you tickle her on her tummy and her feet.
And when the day is over, she says, 'nigh, nigh'
And blows you a kissy as you turn off the light.

Philip Buist (11)

PUDDING LAME

In London a huge Christmas pudding,
blocked every road leading to Tooting,
all those nuts on the road,
were for motorists a goad,
and they all slid around in slime hooting.

Jean Paisley

REFLECTIONS ON A JOURNEY

Travelling by those foreign fields
Across the northern face of France
Seated on a luxury coach
Watching the scenery with a glance.

The miles rolled away endlessly
Field after field of arable land
Picturesque but boring flashed by
With a lonely farm and its hands.

As I saw some cattle grazing
A profound thought occurred to me
What would happen I wondered
If they were taken across the sea?

Could or would they communicate?
What about the language barrier?
Would the English say - 'Ignore those French
Don't talk to them, they're foreigners?'
Or, would the French ones simply say -
'Moo' in a typical French way?

Terry Daley

VALE OF TEARS

A frail Scottish Nationalist from Wick
When at sea was invariably sick.
He would lie in the storage
Disgorging his porridge,
Which was glutinous, gruesome and thick.

An indigent Jain from Madras
Was accustomed to living on grass.
Although chewing the cud
Might discolour the blood
He felt after a while it would pass.

A young weather forecaster from Caen
Got his isobars terribly wrong
When his 'gentle mistral'
Flattened Transalpine Gaul
And caused tidal waves west of Toulon.

The Scottish philosopher, Hume,
Not infrequently yielded to gloom
When the typical weather,
Lashing down on the heather,
Led to pleurisy, foot rot and rheum.

If I were a seagull I'd hover
Where MPs like to think they're Jehovah.
At first signs of a speech
I would cackle and screech
And bombard them with ordure and ova.

When I was an egg in the womb,
I was raring to go: vroom, vroom, vroom.
But, sixty years later
My accelerator
Doesn't work, and it fills me with gloom.

Norman Bissett

SHOCKING SWIM

A group of old women,
Were in the brook swimming.
A rat swam on by,
They started to cry.
And next week they joined up for slimming.

Geoffrey Woodhead

DOT

Ted and Edna wanted a baby, so they performed the baby craft.
The midwife remarked as the child was born, the staff all heard
                                                                            her laugh.

She was such a happy child kindergarten through to school,
Although she was always happy, she was nobody's fool.

In her company, you felt joyous, she's now a happily married mum,
With her own baby daughter she calls Sugar Plum!

She really loves to socialise, drinks wine by the carafe,
That really makes our Dorothy *laugh* and *laugh* and *laugh*.

Ethel Napper

WHOOPS

They used to weigh them by the ounce
and on your lap they would bounce,
Now they weigh them by the gramme
and bounce them in a buggy not a pram,
Up and down, they chuckle on your knee
Agh! When you look the little s . . . 's had a wee,
So once more you try to make them happy
wash and powder another clean nappy.
Oh! Damn, ain't I a silly buggler
now they're posh it's a snuggler,
Cor, when I was a kid it was a towel white
now bums are colour coded, what a sight.
Then friends do calls with ohs and ahs
saying how lovely, a face just like Pa's.
You think and feel very faint
saying to yourself, 'Bl . . . y hell, I hope it ain't.'
Our milkman could get soddin' shot
if my old man notices in his cot.

Edmund Hyde

RIP

A man was sitting up a tree,
'Oh if a bird I could be!'
He flapped his arms, stepped into space
Forgetting he was of the human race -
So, sadly for him - it's - RIP.

Joyce Hockley

SAMSON

Young Sammy Samson was a boy
Who had one aim in life -
To prove that he a strong man was
Like namesake in the Bible.

He grew his hair to give him strength,
But when he went to school
His teacher said, 'Now Sammy boy,
I can't have long-haired louts,
So get it cut at once my lad
Or you will be expelled.'

When asked to put some books away,
He piled them up on high
To prove that he could carry weights
With arms as strong as steel.
Alas! The pile, it swayed, it leaned,
And down it fell with mighty crash
About poor Sammy's feet.

As Sports Day neared, Sam's hopes were high,
There'd be a tug-of-war,
He challenged all his mates to pull
Against his own great strength.
His muscles bulged, he pulled and strained,
To no avail: his feet just slipped
And down he went with painful thump,
Defeated yet again.

There is a moral in this tale
For boastful boys like Sammy.
We can't all be so strong and fierce
And never should we boast,
It only ends in downfall great
And faces red with shame.

Roma Davies

AT HOME WITH HOLMES

'It's good to get home,
This winter's infernal.
I say, Holmes,
Have you seen my journal?

By the way, this morning
I sort of took stock
And would you believe it,
I am missing a sock.'

'Ah! I know where to find that.
It's in my fiddle.
Just poke it out,
It's just pushed in the middle.

Mrs Hudson's a witness,
She heard your demand.
I did put a sock in it,
Yours was to hand.

The sock actually worked,
It improved the tone,
Though when I play again
I'm sure you'll still moan.'

'Holmes, I've searched for your fiddle
And it just isn't there.
I've searched till I'm cold
And I've looked everywhere.

My, that's a good fire,
Upon my very soul.
How does Hudson do it?
We haven't any coal.'

'Haven't any coal? *Mrs Hudson . . .*'
'Holmes, why have you stopped speaking in rhyme?'

R L Cooper

2773

In twenty-seven seventy-three
From a distant Earth colony
Three wise men did come
Bringing gifts by the ton
To Earth, happy people, yippee.

Jokes not heard before see
To set a planet free
From the Christmas cracker jokes
Told by all the Earth folks
Since at least 1986AD.

Like this one of a moon man called Grayey
Thought Mars smelt like Mars bar sweetie
And Pluto smelt of dog
That rolled off a log
And Uranus smelt of . . . smelly feet.

The three men returned to their colony
Said they would return in 2883
But their jokes they did last
Getting laughter ablast
And the Earthlings were freer than free!

H G Griffiths

CAT'S DAYS

He was resting on the wardrobe,
Claws testing out the wood
I asked him to depart, tout time
As friendly as I could

He stared, aloof, with one eye closed
I tried a gentle clout
He landed midst my ironed shirts
And spread them all about.

Roger Brooks

INFINITY

Monkeys typing into infinity
Would produce this poem
And everything else
That had ever been bxyz-oem.

Stan Downing

OVER THE HILL

Too old, too old
So often I'm told
Too old to think or to feel
Too old to reason, create or contribute
These opinions are never concealed

    Too old, too old
    I'm senile I'm told
    By my boss who is twenty-three
    It's alright for him now, but just wait and see
    In six years' time he'll be older than me.

Stuart Delvin

UNTITLED

A man went to the local library, and asked the librarian,
'How long have you been open?'
'Since 1925,' she replied.
'Isn't it time you went for your dinner?' he asked.
'No, I've brought sandwiches,' she answered.

GBC

THE DENTIST

Once there was a dentist,
His name was Doctor White,
He'd find your aching molar
And make it feel alright.

He'd take his demon drill out,
And drill with fiendish glee;
With knee in chest he mutters,
'This hurts you more than me.'

He'll tackle any problem,
He's a specialist in roots,
A quick prick with a needle
And he drills down to your boots.

Cotton wool stuffed in your cheek,
And mouth clamped open wide,
A quick squirt here, a quick squirt there -
He views his work with pride.

Hygienist now is waiting
To polish up your pearls.
Three hundred pounds a visit!
It must be worth it, girls.

Ann Dempsey

DEMONS

We all have our little demons,
The part of us we want to keep locked away,
Because if we were to let it out,
It would be there to stay.

The darker side of our personality,
The side that doesn't show fear,
And speaks its mind,
Who doesn't shed even a tear.

It is the side you've always wanted to be,
Fearless, confident and successful,
Nothing can stand in your way,
You will feel on top of the world, so, so powerful.

However this is just a fantasy,
Reality is a killer to all your dreams,
And the demons stay locked deep down inside,
Hidden away or so it seems.

Kimberly Harries

MISS MAGGIE MACGREE

Miss Maggie Macgree,
To tea
Invited the Abbot uncle Sam.
Sam said thanks by giving grace
For what they were about to receive.
Tuck into bread, butter.
Meat passed and cottage cheese.
Ham, Sam, bread and jam,
In the salad a whopping hairy,
Horned caterpillar.
Sam looked at the monster,
Screamed, 'Kill it.'
Maggie Macgree said, 'It came with the shopping.'
She could not be so cruel,
Suggested, boil down, make an aborigine
Meal of gruel.
Sam remarked,
'That kind of meal makes me ill.'
Maggie took the caterpillar
Into her cottage garden old.
Put the caterpillar on her marigolds;
The whopper ate the lot,
Three rows of shallots,
This, that and the ginger cat
Abbot Uncle Sam
Said, 'I'll be damned.'

B Clarke

THE CHRISTMAS PARTY

I thought I was the smartest girl
that ever set out to a party with
my fully flared red skirt and
blouse to match.

Mum said it was cold out and
gave me a very thick shawl
collar Aron jumper she had
knitted for me to wear until I got there.

Oh! It was a good night with fun,
laughter and drinks aplenty.
Still all good daughters have to
go home in the end, so quickly
pulled on my fine jumper, but
oh dear! Something was very wrong
what can it be? Then I started
to laugh and said out loud,
'I am not drunk, but I have
my jumper on upside down, with
the neck around my waist,' and I
giggled all the way home!

Julia L Holden

A LESSON

In long past school days
A teacher taught with an earnest face:

'Make sure you do not use too much perfume
For otherwise people might assume
That this is meant to cover the undoubted smell
Of not having washed yourself too well.'

M MacDonald-Murray

BEYOND CREDENCE

Produce some rubbish, call it art,
Take the judges by surprise:
A pile of bricks, an unmade bed,
Both have won the Turner Prize.
A light bulb flashing on and off,
You must be joking? No indeed,
The Tate's gone barmy once again
They've nominated Martin Creed!

Corinne Lovell

SWEET BROWN BEAR

I sat next to the sweet brown bear
She looked sweet
As the honey ran down her cheek
Little brown mouse that's shy
Hid under my chair and smiled
As I opened my mouth
My teeth fell out
I blushed from my toes
To my eyes
As the people laughed for hours.

Helen Owen

FINISHED STARTER

Starter motor has gone all-kaput
today's plans have all had to be cut
was upset for a while
till the change brought a smile
for on foot I was out of a rut.

Robert D Shooter

THE REMEDY

If life has no 'rise' for some guys
If their problem is dealing with 'size'
Take a viagra pill
Then go in for the 'kill'
But careful - don't die of surprise!

D M Carne

Party Mayhem

It was the office Christmas party
The boss looked hale and hearty
Then he answered his mobile phone
Choked upon a chicken bone
His face went very, very red
Eyes popping out of his head
Across the room flew his false teeth
And landed on a joint of beef
Recovered he stood tall and big
But caught his watch strap on his wig
By now his staff couldn't hold their laughter back
And thought they'd end up with the sack.

Hazell Dennison

BRIGHT COLOURS OF YOUTH

Gaily painted fingernails
Brightly coloured toes
Used to be just red or pink
Now they're green or golds

In my younger days
Earrings were adorned
Now we tend to see
Naval piercings worn

Tattoos worn by women
Sarongs on the lads
Heads all shaved on girls or guys
Are they all going mad?

Heels that look like great tall birds
Wobbling on their way
And that's just not on the girls
If boys would have their own way

Working mums and housewife dads
Changing over roles
Whatever do the children think
It's all against the rules

I haven't time to worry now
Although it makes me wince
The hairdresser is ready now
To put on my blue rinse

Sonia Riggs

TIME ON MY HANDS

When summertime ends and winter draws near
Then comes the job that I hate every year
Each clock and timer needs to be set
To go back an hour and it's a safe bet
That I never can set them all to be right
It seems to have taken me half of the night
To alter each one, each year there seems more
To remember them all becomes quite a chore
Kitchen clock, cuckoo clock, microwave too
Timer plug, wrist watch to name just a few
The video's worst, I must read the book
Press the wrong button, take a good look
Heating and timing, must get it right
If not it wakes me during the night
Alarm clocks are last as I climb into bed
And gratefully rest my poor weary head
All done again until this time next year -
Then get in the car - there's another one here!

Kath Barber

MONKS ELEIGH

The village where we lived, was the same as all the rest,
With its church, its shops and its bars.
Had a tailor, a butcher, a carpenter too,
And a garage that looked after the cars.

It was quiet in our street, not much happened out there,
While the men-folk spent time on the loam.
Tilling crops that they sewed, which were then raked and hoed,
While their women looked after the home.

It was hard being young, to be poor and survive
In Monks Eleigh, just after the war.
With the cold of that day, which would not go away
And the wolf, to be kept from our door.

In the street where I lived, stood an old water pump
On the green, just across from the school.
Here we'd drink from its spout, where the water gushed out,
Or sometimes we'd just play the fool.

At the top of the hill, stood an ancient old church,
Saint Peter's I think was its name.
Where the parson would pray, here on each new Sunday,
At a service, where very few came.

It was hard in our street, being young as we played,
In the village, or down by the stream.
And now that I'm old, or so I've been told,
So much of it seems like a dream.

All the old folk have gone, from the street where I lived
Now it looks and feels, not the same.
They now rest by the church, 'neath the yew and the birch,
And it's hard to remember their names.

I went back to the house, in the street where I lived,
Although nothing, now looks quite the same.
There are new folk with cars, loud music and bars.
I don't think I'll go back there again.

Richard Lee Nettleton

CHIP-MONK

In any major monastery
The cook has a most important place.
If men renounce the pleasures of the world
The least they can do is feed their face.

One monk who arrived as chief chef
Proved useless as a single bean.
He had no clue as to what to do
And was not even clean.

Soon demoted down to bashing spuds
He chipped those spuds for chips.
Through the Abbot's almost papal edict
He would, on occasion, make cheese dips.

The collective appetite of Friar Tuck hunks
Had the chip-chef at his limit.
His keenness caused the famished monks
To eat the chip-chef-chow: not bin it.

The Abbot had his special fare
A 'ten pound fare' for being transported by throne.
Although I jest, it was very rare
To feed him chips, then for a dare, and that usually alone.

Robert John Moore

THE MAN FROM THE ISLE OF WIGHT

A man from the Isle of Wight
had a belt a bit too tight!
He passed great wind,
his stomach thinned,
gassing everyone in sight!

His wife's brolly was a pain!
Open to both sun and rain!
She was asked why!
Heaved such a sigh!
'But it will be wet again!'

His children adored to eat!
Devouring every treat!
They ate so fast,
it couldn't last!
And vomit covered their feet!

That man, he had a deer,
it was so very queer!
Enormous size!
It had no eyes!
He called it 'No Idea!'

A distant cousin from Crewe
was waiting in a queue!
Wanting some bread!
But got instead
a first-class seat in the loo!

Val Spall

THE ROBIN

The winter sun was shining,
And all the world was still,
I spied a little robin,
Upon my window sill,
I opened up the window,
But it didn't fly away,
It was so tired and hungry,
It had settled there to stay,
I put out lots of breadcrumbs,
To make sure it was fed,
Then I quickly closed the window,
And crushed its little head.

Matthew L Burns

RASPUTIN MADE ME MISS MY BUS!

One morning, while waiting for the bus
I caught a sight oh! Quite stupendous,
for striding down the pavement
and much to my amazement,
swigging from a can of beer
Rasputin did appear!
Verily, that mad Russian monk
looking only slightly drunk,
wore an army surplus parka
and combats a little darker.
His beard flowed, black as tar
as it did in the days of the Tsar,
back when his mesmeric tricks
left the Empress in a fix.
Centre-parted was his hair,
all the way from here to there;
and as he took another swig
I wondered, could it be a wig?
Unluckily for me, this thought
made Rasputin pull up short,
and from over the road he peered
at me - I tell you, I was afeared!
Into mine his eyes were bored
as hypnotised and overawed
I was totally in his power.
Then upon the stroke of the hour
for once on time, my bus sped past
and I was as you'd expect, aghast
to know that morning, I'd be late
because Rasputin had got on my plate.

Jonathan Goodwin

OLD COMPANIONS

Sue had a pair of pet monkeys which died the same day,
even though expensive she decided to have them stuffed anyway.
The taxidermist said, 'Would you like them mounted Sue?'
She said, 'No, just holding hands will do.'

Brian Bates

THE DIET

I'll lose some weight, decision made
and all those well thought plans are laid.

No cakes or biscuits will be bought,
diet will be the food for thought.

No chips or fries, just grills from now,
it seems the thing to do somehow.

The family moan, we aren't too fat
and really we don't fancy that.

But steadfastly I'll stand my ground
and maybe lose just one more pound.

I'll stick it out, those clothes will meet,
meanwhile I'll just have one more sweet.

Christine Lannen

THE ROOKIE

The raw recruits at naval base
Stood awkward and unsure,
As before them strode, back straight as board,
Drill instructor - Matt McLure.

Now in this rank and file of men
A red face did appear,
McLure stared hard across the yard
At rookie, Jimmy Weir.

'What 'ave we 'ere? What 'ave we 'ere?'
The instructor bellowed loud
At the tardy lad in disarray
Who stood red-faced and bowed.

'You piece of poo! What time do you
Call this, you 'orrible bloke?'
'Six o'clock Sir,' spoke the lad.
McLure winced as he spoke.

'You're in the Navy now, mi lad,
In Navy terms we speak.
Now answer me in 'nautical'
Or you're grounded for a week!'

The young lad sighed - the instructor roared
'This ain't no birthday party!'
The raw recruit yelled, loud and clear . . .
'Six o'clock . . . mi hearty!'

Linda Zulaica

You're Sunk Mate!

I heard a sailor call to me
While he was swimming in the sea.

His ship had struck a floating mine,
So he called out, 'Drop me a line.'

I couldn't do so, I confess -
I didn't know this chap's address!

Roger Williams

JED'S PARROT

As a birthday gift, a parrot Jed received
But its language was crude, which constantly peeved
Jed tried many ways to change the bird
But miserably failed as more swearing occurred
Finally, quite desperate, Jed took the bird in his hand
Put it in the freezer, and for a minute did stand
The bird squawked, kicked and screamed, at first
Then suddenly went quiet - into the freezer Jed burst
Fearing his method too drastic, he anxiously peered in
But the parrot calmly stepped out, saying, 'Okay, you win
I'm truly sorry I've offended, with language so crude
My actions too, I know have been rude
I will endeavour at once my behaviour to correct
I beg your forgiveness, with utmost respect.'
Jed was astonished at the dramatic change in his bird
He was about to ask what, in the freezer, occurred
When the parrot continued, still perched on the lid
'May I ask what it was that the chicken did?'

Mary Wood

GIVE THAT TUNE THE BRUSH OFF!

Rooney had a tune that kept going round his head.
Around it went no matter what else was done or said.
He tried to drown it by turning his walkman up high,
But that only brought complaints from passers-by.
He tried simple things like stuffing cotton wool into his ears,
His sister laughed so much that she ended up in tears.
Rooney thought, what can I do to make this tune go away?
I really need to stop it, if only for one day.
He tried sitting in the dark with a paper bag over his head,
But the rustling of the bag annoyed him more instead.
He tried singing all the time, though he couldn't sing a note.
He had to give it up when he got a really sore throat.
He went to the doctor who 'ummed' and 'aahed',
'I really don't know - this case is just too hard.'
He sent Rooney to a specialist in ear, nose and throat.
Rooney wondered what was written in the doctor's note.
The specialist burst out laughing and said, 'Excuse me!
I can cure you but £25 will be payable as my fee.'
'Anything - I'm desperate!' Rooney replied.
'Okay, put your right arm out and lie on your left side.'
The specialist tickled Rooney's face, nose and ear with a brush.
When Rooney finished laughing all he could hear was a hush.
Joyfully he wiped his eyes, smiled and shook his head.
'It always works, don't ask me to explain it,' the specialist said.
Yes, the secret's out, but don't be like Rooney and have to pay,
Keep a small, soft brush handy in case that tune comes your way.

Rosina L Gutcher

THE WEDDING

The car taking bride to town
A mile from the church, broke down
She had a ride in a cart
Reaching church late and not smart.

Mother cried and Father swore
And said, 'Now troubles galore'
The parson had a sore throat
Organ missed many a note.

The best man then lost the ring
Thought it was a funny thing
Trouble above and below
Why? Nobody seemed to know.

A reception to a marquee
They all went quite eagerly
Father to his ire gave vent
Marquee was only a tent.

At last there was some order
Bride and groom off to border
With a nice fine honeymoon
They were both over the moon.

Peter Arthur Butcher

GO ON! JUST ONE MORE!

When you're young, small and round
Having fun and piling on pounds
No one tells you to beware
If you carry on you'll explode, go bang
Or break a chair!
Another cake, go on, it's there
Stuff in a slice or chocolate éclair
Bend your knees, raise your arms
Roll around and get all warm
Release some wind, grunt and groan!
Burn off that cake and make some room
There's another course ready to eat,
Or even a bag of lovely sweets!
How much more can I fit in, one, two or even three,
There's enough for you and enough for me
Thank goodness this day arrives, just once a year
A day when all you do is eat, it would appear!
At least my conscience will soon be clear,
With the arrival of a brand new year!

Angela Jones

THE BOAR

Father pig instructing his noisy brood,
'Now keep still, listen and don't be rude.'
They reply, 'We can't keep still anymore,
Because dear Dad . . . you are a bore.'

Valerie Ovais

A TWIST TO THE TALE

Dogs are my preference but cats are all right
Except unless neutered they want out at night,
Which can be a nuisance, so have the beast spayed
If you ever possess one, it can't be delayed.
Especially with female pussies around
Think of the caterwauling, terrible sound.

A good friend who didn't like neutering much
Had a black and white Tom, which resulted in such
An awful commotion when kittens appeared
Her neighbours protesting just as I feared.
'There are other Toms,' she wailed, quite pathetic
But the proof of the pudding was really genetic.

One cat in each litter had a twist to its tail,
Identification, now no one could fail
To know which Tom sired them, a defect all had,
Surely inherited, came from their dad.
Paternity now could not be denied
However much my unhappy friend tried.
Her cat's tail was twisted and had been from birth.
A tale which created a great deal of mirth.

Ellen Thompson

INFORMATION

We hope you have enjoyed reading this book - and that you will continue to enjoy it in the coming years.

If you like reading and writing poetry drop us a line, or give us a call, and we'll send you a free information pack.

Write to :-
**Triumph House Information
Remus House
Coltsfoot Drive
Peterborough
PE2 9JX
(01733) 898102**